# A PLACE TO HIDE

"Mindset is the foundation of self-defense. This book is a great read on situational awareness, and the deep dive on threat assessment is spot on. Always have a plan to get out!"

—AIMEE GRANT
*Firearms Instructor, Field Editor,*
*Contributor to American Handgunner*

"The greatest defensive skill is awareness. Mc-Shaffrey's book is a must read for everyone, whether they choose to be armed or not. The best fight is the one we avoid."

—JIM WILSON
*Former Texas Sheriff,*
*Contributor to Shooting Illustrated*

"A Place to Hide provides the mindset needed to respond appropriately instead of freezing, since preparedness results in clearer thinking when you find yourself in such a dangerous situation."

—BETH WARFORD
*Founder and Owner: Pretty Loaded*

"Sadly, our culture is changing quickly... one public shooting after another seems to fill the headlines. McShaffrey's book will help you and your loved ones make crucial decisions no matter where the next dangerous outbreak takes place."

—MATTHEW EVERHARD
*Author, Pastor of Gospel Fellowship*
*Presbyterian Church*

# A PLACE TO HIDE

*Equipping Ordinary Moms To Survive A Public Shooting*

CHRISTIAN MCSHAFFREY

Kept Pure Press

ISBN (paperback): 979-8-218-40828-2
ISBN (e-book): 979-8-218-40829-9

Dedicated to the late Janelle Cooper, faithful wife of Col. Jeff Cooper and mother of three daughters, who was so kind as to serve me a homemade brownie and a cold Arnold Palmer at the family "Sconce" on a warm Friday afternoon.

# Contents



## SECTION ONE: PRINCIPLES

## SECTION TWO: PRACTICUM

# Disclaimer

The insights and advice offered in this book come from an admitted "non-expert" in public safety and tactical training.

He has done plenty of study, and also received some firearm training, but holds no certificate or license that qualifies him to instruct others.

This book is for educational or informational purposes only and should not be considered a substitute for professional advice, consultation with professionals, or professional training.

# Preface

As is my custom, I sat sipping my coffee and browsing the news headlines on an average weekday morning. There had been another public shooting. This time, it happened during a parade.

A decade ago, I would have clicked on the headline to see what exactly had happened, how many were dead or injured, and whether the police had apprehended a suspect or discerned any possible motives. On this particular day, however, I simply sighed and said a silent prayer.

Praying is good. I recommend it to all who have faith, but I have also always been interested in more immediate matters of the practical sort (especially as a husband and father).

My wife and children happened to be traveling that same week to visit grandma for her birthday. They were, thankfully, nowhere near the shooting,

but even if they had been, I would not have panicked because I have taught them over the years
how to stay safe in an increasingly insane world.

I am typing this two days after the incident,
and since I mentioned it in the preface, I wanted
to revisit the story to see if there were any developments.

Apparently, one mother was killed, and twenty-
two people were injured, nine of whom were
children.

There is nothing I can do to help them, but I
may be able to help you by sharing what I have
learned over the years about staying safe in public
spaces.

Christian McShaffrey

February 16, 2024

Midwest, USA

# Introduction

This book will probably be unlike any other you have ever read. That is not because I intend it to be so. The material which follows comes most naturally to my mind, but not everyone thinks like me. I know that and am comfortable enough with the fact.

I grew up in a different era. There was no such thing as mass shootings at schools or parades. At least, if there was such a thing, I was blissfully unaware of it. My friends and I played outside all day long in the summer and were not expected home until the street lights came on.

Like most boys back then, we rode our dirt bikes—yes, on the streets!—until we could disappear into the fields and woods. There, we built forts, foraged for wild berries, caught fish, trapped rabbits, captured the flag, and felt like men.

The Boy Scouts' periodical "Boy's Life" helped us hone our skills. I also still have a well-worn copy of "Tom Brown's Field Guide to Wilderness Survival" somewhere in the basement. This guide taught me how to eat toxic plants like milkweed.

These adolescent desires to survive in the dangerous wild eventually matured, but the "spirit to survive" always remained. It just adapted to new life circumstances.

When a man starts a family, his responsibilities change. His mentality undergoes a significant shift. His thoughts are no longer limited to, "What would *I* do in this situation?" Now they have to be, "What would *we* do?"

My wife doesn't think like me. I remember, for example, driving our minivan across a dilapidated bridge on Interstate 80 several years ago, and I asked the family, "What would you do if the bridge collapsed right now and our van plummeted into the icy river below?"

To me, the answer is simple: Brace for impact, remove seat belts once afloat, help the smaller children to get unbuckled, open the windows before the electronics failed, exit the vehicle, and start swimming for shore.

I can imagine what you might be thinking. "What?!" Again, not everyone thinks like me. Most people don't "run scenarios" in the back of their mind while driving. Some do, however, and you can benefit from it.

In section one of this book, I will teach you a variety of principles related to situational awareness, avoiding risky situations, what happens to your mind and body when danger arises, options for finding cover, and what you will experience while hiding.

No, these are not pleasant points to ponder, but if taken to heart, they will serve you well if you ever find yourself in a life-threatening situation.

In section two, I will offer practical advice for staying safe in various environments. I personally visited most of the locations mentioned in this book with a clipboard in hand. When able, I spoke with a manager or employee and determined the safest places to hide in each location.

After completing my manuscript, I asked a military combat veteran, a city police officer, a county sheriff, and several moms to review it. All of their input has been incorporated.

Therefore, what you hold in your hands is all

you probably need to know about avoiding and surviving a public shooting event.

# Section One: Principles

You purchased this book because you want to survive—not just in general, but in *specific* situations, such as those already mentioned.

There might be a temptation to flip to the more *practical* pages of this book. And hey, if you are going to Walmart later today, by all means, read that section first.

At the same time (as with all learned skills), fundamental principles always come first.

If you master the material in this first section, you will understand the practical section much better. In fact, you will probably be able to make all the assessments in section two yourself.

Be patient, learn the material, and all the

*practical matters* will make perfect sense in the end.
I promise.

# Situational Awareness

Being aware of your surroundings is the first step toward staying safe in any given environment. Experts call this "situational awareness," which is simply a matter of paying attention to what is around you and adjusting your mental disposition as those things change.

I was first inclined to explain the process of potential mental adjustments in terms of a traffic light because that would be easy enough for most people to remember:

- Green: Relax, all is well
- Yellow: Pay attention, something's off
- Red: Act now, your life is at risk

If that makes sense to you, then go ahead and use it. You will be more aware of your circumstances and more able to adjust your mental condition than most people are.

The only problem with that illustration is that the "yellow" category is too vague. We need to add another color, and as you might have guessed, it is going to be orange.

I first learned the "four color codes" of situational awareness and mental condition from an old black-and-white video recording of Col. Jeff Cooper (1920–2006). You can probably still find it on the Internet. What follows is a brief summary.

## Condition White: Oblivious

This is the condition in which most of us would prefer to live our lives each day.

For a guy like me, condition white would look something like a quiet Sunday afternoon on my homestead, sitting on the couch reading a good book, my dog napping on the front porch, and my pistol sitting on the coffee table.

For a mom like you, it might be a quiet Saturday afternoon, with a warm bath drawn, some scented candles burning, and the steady hum of your husband's riding mower in the distance.

Those who have intentionally created "safe

spaces" for themselves deserve to spend time within them while in condition white, but they must also be ready to make a mental shift to code yellow as circumstances change.

## Condition Yellow: Aware

This mental state is only a small step away from white. If, for example, you are soaking in the tub and you hear the UPS truck coming down the driveway, your mind will naturally shift from being oblivious to being aware, but it will be a *relaxed* awareness. After all, your overly protective husband is out there mowing the lawn. This is code yellow.

Col. Cooper said, "You can stay in yellow for the rest of your life" because it involves no specific alarm or threat. It is just the mental state of being consciously aware of your surroundings and always being ready to shift to the next level of awareness if necessary.

Just so you know, living by the four color code can sometimes make going out to lunch with new friends a little awkward. Whenever the hostess shows us to our table, I always take the seat that best enables me to see the whole dining room, especially the front door.

Do people sometimes notice? Might some think it strange? Undoubtedly. But if anything bad ever happened while dining with us in public, they will probably prove grateful for this personal idiosyncrasy in the end.

Stay aware. That's code yellow. Don't be anxious, but calmly scan your surroundings, identify the exits, and glance up whenever new customers enter. This will leave you perfectly equipped to respond if a "yellow" situation escalates into an "orange" situation.

## Condition Orange: Alert

While code yellow is a mental state of *relaxed* awareness, a shift into code orange becomes necessary when a new and specific element is added to the situation.

Think back to our lunch date, for example. If a waiter drops a tray, or someone starts yelling, or a street gang enters through the doors, your state of relaxed awareness should immediately be heightened to a *focused* awareness. You are now on alert.

If the noise indeed was just a dropped tray, you

can quickly shift back into code yellow once they start sweeping up the mess. With the other examples, however, code orange is where your mind needs to stay until the specific disruption or distraction is resolved.

By the way, be mindful of how you appear to others as you actively monitor your environment. Practice the fine art of observing without staring. Prolonged eye contact can be intimidating and can sometimes agitate the wrong person.

Just keep your eyes open. Keep them focused on whatever seems "off," and start thinking about what you would do if you needed to act. Yes, you have just started running scenarios in your mind. Welcome to the club!

I say that somewhat in jest because I realize I may have ruined your next date night. Rather than gazing into your lover's eyes, you will now be scanning the room. Don't worry, though. You can do both. Again, you could live your whole life in yellow.

Code orange is, obviously, way more intense, but in most cases, it is only temporary. An *actual* threat either materializes or does not. If it doesn't, then go ahead and enjoy your meal. If it does, the meal is over, and it is time to move.

## Condition Red: Action

Quick review: We started in white mode, which was a happy state of oblivion. Safe within the confines of our own homes, we can sometimes "tune out" and give little thought to what's happening outside.

Then, however, we walked the dog, took the kids to the park, dropped off books at the library, went out to lunch, and that necessitated a shift to code yellow (i.e., a *relaxed* awareness of our surroundings and strangers present).

If, in one of those imagined situations, something doesn't seem right, or something gets loud, or something goes wrong, you shift into code orange. Your awareness is now laser-focused on a *specific* potential threat.

Again, a genuine threat will not materialize most of the time, but if and when it does, you need to respond and take immediate action. This is code red, time to act.

Of course, what *exactly* that action should be depends on the circumstances and could include a variety of things like running, hiding, fighting, calling the police, etc.

The first thing you should do, however, applies to almost every imaginable situation: Get down! More on this later.

It is not so much our interest in this section to explore these options as it has been simply to explain the four categories of situational awareness that determine your mental state.

Obviously, no one ever wants to be in a code red condition. Sometimes, it is inevitable, but thankfully, it is oftentimes *avoidable*. We will consider this in the next chapter.

# Avoiding Risk

You've heard the old adage, "The best offense is a good defense." That may be true enough in the sporting world, but I would suggest a better saying in our real world of unchecked crime and cruel predation. Namely, "Avoidance is better than either offense or defense."

It has been a week since I began writing this book, and I decided to check back on the parade shooting news coverage to see if there were any new developments. Sure enough, there were. Two "juveniles" were charged, and videos were even released that showed part of the conflict that instigated the shooting. The footage even showed some of the action and the aftermath.

Engaging in speculative forensics is far beyond the scope of this book, so let me draw your attention to something one of the witnesses said: "It looked a little sketchy, and then you just heard shots. And then I looked and I saw a body right there and a body right there..."

First of all, notice how quickly a scene can go from looking "a little sketchy" to having dead bodies strewn about on the ground.

This is why memorizing and practicing the mental color codes is so important. Live your life in yellow. Shift in and out of orange as necessary. But the *second* a situation goes red, you must be ready to act. We will come back to that, though, in due time.

Our focus, for now, is *avoiding* unnecessary risk, and it is not that complicated. At the same time, it requires some patterns of thought that the sophisticates of our day might consider politically incorrect. I will do my best to describe it in a non-offensive manner.

Some people pose more risk than others. Some events present more of a potential risk than others. Ignore these obvious facts, and it may be to your peril.

For example, back in the 19th century, there existed an undesirable class of citizens called *hooligans.* I have some Irish ancestry, so I think it's safe enough for me to talk about them.

The word "hooligan" seems to trace back to a particularly rowdy Irish clan whose only contribution to London was a gang of "juveniles" known as the *O'Hooligan Boys.* Their name still lives on, but only as a slur for those who cause social unrest.

Whatever you choose to call them today, and whatever ancestry they happen to share, there are still groups of young men who spend most of their time loitering, drinking, smoking, fighting, stealing, and looking for ordinary people to harass and harm.

Stay away from them. That is the simplest way to avoid risk. Identify the "high risk" people in your area, determine when and where they tend to congregate, and stay clear of them.

This, admittedly, may require some sacrifice on your part. Your children may even protest on occasion.

For example, the violent event that spurred me to write this book occurred at a parade. Who doesn't love a parade? I do, and I take my family to one every single summer.

However, if you are enjoying that parade in

your mental state of code yellow and, while scanning the scene, see a bunch of hooligans coming together in one area, you now have a choice to make.

You could shift to code orange and keep an alert eye on that section of the crowd, or you could justifiably shift to code red, quickly retreat, and go back home.

Will your children complain? Undoubtedly. But just consider: how many people wish they could go back in time and rethink their attendance at that parade, which so quickly and unexpectedly turned into a proverbial war zone?

"Better safe than sorry" is another proverb you should probably engrave upon your heart. Disappointing those we love is an infinitely better option than *losing* those we love.

Having now covered your personal mental state and the priority of avoiding danger whenever possible, we will now proceed to principles that apply when a condition orange situation is about to go red.

# Alerting Authorities

The police force exists to keep people safe. Don't wait until a situation goes all the way to red before calling for their assistance. The *moment* you stop feeling safe, simply dial 911 and say so.

You also need to remember a very real limitation called *response time*. That's the average time it takes between dialing 911 and actually seeing the police arrive. This time varies from district to district, so I can't tell you what yours might be. Call the dispatcher (on the non-emergency line!) and ask. They might be able to give you an estimate.

The main point here is obvious: The sooner, the better. Call for help *before* you think you need it.

In an upcoming chapter, you will learn about several options for hiding from an active threat. Obviously, you can't make any noise while hiding, so make sure you know how to silence your cell phone quickly.

Once silenced, dial 911 and keep it simple. Say something like, "I'm at Pineview School and there's a shooter." That's all they need to know. Hang up and get quiet again.

Fair warning: The dispatcher will call you back, but staying safe is more important than answering.

Some departments may even be able to find your location because of modern technology and the ever-expanding networks of data sharing. But don't count on it.

If you cannot call 911 because doing so would compromise your hiding spot, text the person who is most likely to receive and respond the quickest.

One additional option that will work on many phones is the "SOS" feature. Take a few minutes to learn how this future works on your phone because it is designed to call 911 (or your local emergency services) automatically. Some phones will even tell you to "Stay calm" while you are waiting.

Again, the authorities exist to keep you safe. Alert them immediately as soon as you begin feeling unsafe. No, it is not a good feeling, but it happens, and it is essential that you understand what it's like. Hence, my next chapter.

# Flight or Fight

Surely, you've been startled before. You know what it feels like: your body tenses up, you stop breathing for a second, your heart begins racing, and maybe you get a little shaky.

Usually, those feelings subside rather quickly as you realize there is no true threat at hand. You were just surprised and became startled.

Imagine, however, that these feelings are *not* resolved. Sometimes, they *can't* resolve because there is actually a threat at hand. Your brain senses this and triggers what the specialists call our "flight or fight" response.

This is an entirely biological process to perceived threats, meaning it is perfectly involuntary. You *will* experience it in a code red situation. Let me highlight some of the most common physical effects so that you are not surprised:

- Increased heart rate
- Rapid breathing
- Skin going pale
- Dilation of the eyes

All these reactions are related. Your sympathetic nervous system has perceived a threat and is preparing all your body parts for immediate action.

The increased heart and breathing rate increases the flow of highly oxygenated blood to your brain and main muscle groups, which is why you become pale. Your eyes dilate to capture increased light so you can see more of your surroundings and avenues for escape.

All of this is perfectly natural and to be expected. No, it does not *feel* good, but it does serve us well as we are forced to choose between the two options: flight or fight.

I honestly wish there were more options, but there are not. Again, our instincts have already come to terms with that, so our feelings must catch up with reality.

Many people wrongly focus on their personality

or general disposition when considering whether to fight or flee. True, some people are natural fighters, and others are not, but that has nothing to do with making the choice.

For example, I have something of a fighting spirit, but my first preference in a code red situation would always be to flee—especially if my wife and children are with me.

On the other hand, my wife is not a fighter at all. She wouldn't hurt a fly. But if some stranger grabbed her baby, I'm sure the world would see an entirely different side of her.

Our choice between flight and fight depends not on our personality but on the present *circumstances*. Remember, you are already well aware of those because you have been operating in a mental state of awareness and ever-increasing alertness.

Now, your brain is calling for action. It has already equipped your organs and muscles to take that action. So make a decision and get out of the situation as quickly as possible.

Some might wonder, "But what about the *fight* option?" It is a legitimate question, but for the purpose of this book, I have chosen to focus only on the flight option. Fighting is off the table for now.

I did not make that decision because fighting is a poor choice. I carry a concealed firearm every day and am trained to use it. I am, as they say, "Armed and ready" if the need should arise.

Some of you may eventually become interested in learning how to carry and use a concealed weapon. But I can't teach you how to do that responsibly in a book. It requires hands-on training, time at the shooting range, practice, accountability, and the development of muscle memory.

Besides that, as I already admitted, I would much rather *sneak* out of a dangerous situation than *shoot* myself out of one. Most mature firearm owners would agree.

From this point on, we will therefore focus only on the non-engagement option of self-defense in a public shooting situation.

We will start with a concept called "cover," which essentially consists of finding ways to hide yourself from harm.

# Finding Cover

Before I sat down to write today, I returned to news updates about the recent parade shooting. While I did not intend it to function as such, the event is slowly becoming something of a case study.

I watched a newsreel that included comments from those who witnessed the shooting. One mom said, "We literally heard it right behind us, and they said, 'active shooter,' and we just started running."

That, as we learned in the previous chapter, is precisely what our biological "flight response" enables us to do. I am guessing that particular mom ran faster than she had in a very long time.

Good for her, but I also can't help but wonder (and I wish I could ask her), "In what direction did you run and why? Was there a destination? Or did you just start running?"

This is where our built-in "flight response" is woefully insufficient as a mere instinct. Yes, our brain and body know to flee, but that's a pretty base instinct, and we could definitely benefit from some basic instruction.

Therefore, the new topic is "cover," which is anything you can put between yourself and the perceived threat. There are a few types to consider.

## Natural Cover

If I asked you to name some bullet-proof items, you would probably think first of army tanks, soldier helmets, police vests, bank glass, etc. That may seem perfectly natural, but it actually *ignores* nature.

Most trees are bullet-proof, even the smaller ones that you could never climb. Dirt is bullet-proof, especially in the form of a berm. Water can be bullet-proof if you swim a few feet below the surface.

Many things in the environment can effectively hide you from a dangerous person and potentially even stop a bullet from striking you.

These sources of natural cover are part of what you should be scanning, noticing, and remembering when in a code yellow or orange situation.

In addition to doing a thorough inventory of immediately available natural cover, you should also mentally prioritize the options according to how close they are to you, how quickly you could get behind them, and how bullet-proof they actually are.

By the way, all this assumes that you know the source of the threat. You probably know if you conducted a code orange survey of your environment, but even if not, it is usually easy enough to determine.

Remember the previously mentioned mom who just "started running" when she heard the gunfire? Don't forget that she also included the phrase "behind us" while recalling the event, which means her instincts were tuned in enough to the situation to afford her crucial information.

If your instincts are not that in tune, just take a quick look around, identify the nearest commotion, and do your best to ensure your chosen cover stands between you and it.

## Man-made Cover

One of the benefits of living in our industrialized society is that there is no shortage of man-made cover in public places. Just look for timber, metal, and concrete. It is, quite literally, all over the place.

**Timber**—These are wooden posts and boards used to build structures. You might see, for example, plenty of cedar fences in your town, but these are not thick enough to stop a bullet. A lot of timber is only sufficient to *conceal* you, but more on that later.

Most picnic tables, on the other hand, are made of thicker lumber and would function as very effective cover. You must tip it on its side, but that can be done quickly enough.

**Metal**—Take a short walk down the main street of your town and look for things made of steel. You will probably find postal drop-off boxes, utility boxes near intersections or stop lights, and plenty of steel doors. All of these should be able to stop a bullet.

Let's also not overlook one of the most accessible forms of steel cover around: vehicles. They are all over the place, and the engines within them will definitely stop a bullet.

If you use a vehicle as cover, crouch behind the front tire. In addition to the engine, you will have a steel rim protecting your body, and an attacker will not be able to see your feet (if they even bother to look beneath the vehicle).

The same goes for another oft-overlooked source of public cover: dumpsters. And don't worry, I'm not going to advise you to jump into one because that would cut off all avenues of escape. Just sneak behind one if needed; plenty of steel will be between you and the source of danger.

**Concrete**—There is no shortage of concrete in our towns, and most of it will stop a bullet.

In addition to apparent concrete structures like buildings and retaining walls, look for less obvious structures like planting beds and the large bases at the bottom of street lights. All of these are solid enough to use as personal cover.

If you have a child with you, always put them into cover first; you can then snuggle up behind them. This way, the child benefits from "double cover" thanks to your self-sacrificial love. This position will also enable you to keep them quiet and still as you hide. Again, more on that later.

Speaking of children, though, don't overlook fire hydrants. Yes, they are small, but they are sufficient for a toddler. I might even hug one if there were no other options around.

Speaking of no other options, let's now address the "worst-case scenario" regarding cover. There is none!

## No cover?

First of all, are you sure? Let's be honest about how rare a case this would be. If you were running a relay in a track tournament, there would appear to be no cover nearby, but there is almost always *some* cover to be found.

Even a recessed spot on the ground can serve as sufficient cover because being on the ground actually changes everything.

Shooters, you see, look for targets, and the more conspicuous they are, the better. Moving targets are always the first to attract a shooter's attention because shooters tend to scan their field of vision while looking down the barrel of a rifle, which is typically positioned nearly parallel to the ground.

This is just a natural posture based on instinct, and it takes some special training to convince the eyes to look in unnatural or inconvenient directions.

I mean, when was the last time you looked up into a tree without having a reason to do so (like hearing a bird sing)? Likewise, when was the last time you looked down without something attracting your attention?

The main point is this: Get down on the ground the moment you hear gunfire. This makes you "smaller" as a target and may even leave you completely out of sight to the untrained shooter.

And yes, this means you may need to *crawl* toward cover. No, it's not comfortable, but it increases your chances of survival exponentially.

One more thing you need to consider as an option is what we call *improvised* cover.

For example (and don't ask me how I know this), an iPad will stop a .40 caliber bullet at short range. You can also purchase very nice backpack and briefcase inserts online made from the same material used in police vests.

There is almost always *something* you can place between you and a shooter.

I once heard the testimony of a soldier who had a bullet stop halfway through the small Bible he was carrying in his breast pocket. I'm not sure I believe it, but good for him. Get creative and stay alive.

Finally, there is one last source of improvised cover that would never cross the mind of a civilian but is used by soldiers every single day: smoke.

By the way, military manuals will call smoke *concealment* rather than *cover*, so feel free to do your own "deep dive" into the subject if interested. I'm conflating the two concepts because this book is for moms, not Marines.

Soldiers use smoke grenades to create a quick smoke screen, but such devices are not available to average citizens like us. That is no problem. All you need is a lighter and some flammable material. And yes, you should start carrying a lighter in your purse.

Setting your hiding place ablaze will probably feel counterintuitive, but there are unquestionable benefits to obscuring your existing cover even further.

First, if the shooter is looking for easy targets

of opportunity, walking into a fire zone will seem very unappealing.

Secondly, your fire may trigger the alarm and sprinkler system in a building. This confounds the shooter, which makes him less effective, and automatically alerts first responders to the emergency.

So go ahead, light a garbage can on fire. Move it under the curtains, generate lots of smoke, and get down—not only because it is your go-to position for safety, but because it is the only place you will be able to breathe once the smoke begins to spread.

Having identified a variety of cover options, we also need to be honest about some of their limitations.

# Degrees of Cover

Not all cover is created equal, obviously. Some may seem sketchy at first glance. That's fine, as long as you understand the different *degrees* of cover and the inherent strengths and weaknesses of each.

## Obscurement

Now, we are starting to get into the weeds a bit. No, literally! Weeds can be a great source of cover (especially if they are tall) but only of a particular kind of cover: obscurement.

Obscurement means making yourself *indistinct*, and it is all a matter of perspective.

Consider, for example, crouching behind a bush or decorative grass. You can probably still see the shooter, and he could most likely find you if he really tried, but this is ordinarily beyond the scope of his focus. Shootings happen fast, and most shooters move fast.

Anything you can find that will obscure your silhouette is better than standing out in the open. Obscure yourself.

## Concealment

You could also call this position being *heavily* obscured. The previously mentioned cedar fence would be a prime example. It may not be able to stop a bullet, but it does not need to because it is simply not an attractive target to a shooter.

The only "catch" to concealment is that you cannot efficiently operate from behind cover without revealing your position. Any movement out of concealment may be noticed, so keep that in mind as you are tempted to "peek out" to see what's happening or, perhaps, to relocate to better cover.

If you do choose to relocate, take your time. Don't try to get there all at once. Visualize the path you will take and move maybe 25 yards at a time. If you have never crawled that far, trust me, you will want to stop and catch your breath occasionally.

Besides that, safely arriving at increasingly

better cover will help your mental state. Go ahead and celebrate the small victory of having "made it" to your next position.

## Hiding

Obscurement makes you nondescript. Concealment makes you practically invisible. Hiding takes it to a whole other level.

Most of you will remember playing "hide and seek" as a child. Some were better at the game than others.

There was always that one kid who would just slip behind the curtains, crouch behind the couch, or crawl under a bed. They would always be the first to be found—remember?

Then, there was that other kid who would crawl inside the washing machine, into the kitchen cabinets, or even sneak out of the house ever-so-quietly and safely watch the game unfold from outside. I remember hating that kid. Now, in retrospect, I kind of envy him.

It's not easy to hide yourself completely, but it is a legitimate approach to utilizing cover. The benefit, of course, is complete concealment. This keeps you out of sight until your cover is blown.

Keep in mind that most public shooters are *not* going to slow down and start looking into cabinets in search of a target. You are extremely safe in there.

There is, however, also a disadvantage to this approach: Not only can the shooter *not* see you, but you can also *not* see him. Any attempt to do so might allow him to see you.

So you need to think before choosing this option. In some ways, it is the best. You are no longer visible. In other ways, it is highly challenging because you are now entirely in the dark and need to stay perfectly silent and still.

If you were playing hide-and-seek, the thrill of winning is enough to settle your restlessness. In a life-or-death situation, though, there is no thrill of winning. Everything is wrong. Nothing is as it should be, preventing most people from remaining still for very long. So, let's go ahead and be honest about our inherent antsiness.

Whether you have availed yourself of obscurement, concealment, or an absolute hiding form of cover, there will come a moment when you begin to wonder, "Should I move? Is there better cover?

Is the attack over? What if the shooter is coming my way?" This leads us to the next topic.

# Do I Stay or Go?

Just as Col. Cooper said that we could live our whole lives in yellow, I suggest that we could spend an entire conflict behind cover.

The only people required to leave cover are those who choose to fight back. If you need to return fire or want to provide suppressing fire for someone else, then yes, you will need to expose yourself.

But again, this book is for you, moms. It is written under the assumption that you do not have a weapon or that if you do, you do not intend to engage because you have children with you.

If you are not prepared to engage, don't. It is as simple as that. Remain behind your chosen cover unless you need to move. Then again, that's easier said than done.

Any movement out of cover or toward better cover must be executed carefully. You truly do need to be as sly as a fox. This includes staying low, moving slowly, and staying absolutely alert all the while.

If your movement is detected, you are now at a serious disadvantage, and you might even be in grave danger.

Reading these things on paper is easy. I trust it all makes immediate sense to you, but again, all of this is easier said than done because of what medical professionals call "the state of shock."

For example, let's say your dinner date is interrupted by an armed robbery, and you are forced to flee back into the kitchen. Hiding under a countertop or behind a cabinet might be a perfectly sufficient option. That is, until it's not because you hear someone entering the kitchen.

You may need to move into a pantry or a walk-in freezer. That's fine; do what you need to do, but "sly as a fox" remains the name of the game.

Even *after* you are fully hidden, your silence and stillness must persevere, but this will become increasingly difficult due to the onset of shock.

Even after things quiet down, how do you

know when it is safe to come out? Worse, what if you hear someone opening doors throughout the kitchen? Is it the police? Is it the attacker? You can't know, so your mind will start racing, and so will your heart rate. All of this is perfectly natural.

Medics call it "shock," and it is just as biologically inevitable as our "flight or fight" response. Let me try to prepare you for it in the next chapter.

# Preparing for Shock

I have only been in shock a couple of times. My earliest memory was when I was bringing groceries in for my mom. I was probably nine years old.

A Coca-Cola bottle hit the floor, exploded, and shot a shard of glass into my leg. Blood was gushing out. I became lightheaded and didn't remember anything after praying in the car on the way to the hospital.

The other time was when I crushed my finger in a log splitter. It didn't hurt, but after I removed my glove, looked at the damage, and asked my friend to drive me to the emergency room, everything started to change.

Shock does strange things to the mind and body. Here are a few of the most common symptoms:

- Cool, pale, clammy skin

- Bluish tinge to lips and fingernails
- Rapid pulse and/or breathing
- Nausea, shaking, weakness
- Dilated pupils

If you remember, these symptoms overlap somewhat with what we already learned about pre-conflict biological responses. That's because our body prioritizes the same things before, during, and after a conflict (i.e., our vital organs and main muscle groups).

While completely natural, this state of mind and body is not something we usually experience. Therefore, it can be quite unsettling.

For example, if you try to use your cell phone to call for help while crouching behind cover, you may notice that your fingers are not typing well. Your thoughts may also be frustrated. "What's the police station's number?" Just dial 911.

Feelings of shock may also prompt you to blow your cover prematurely. The phrase, "I just can't take it anymore!" has been heard in more than one foxhole and led to the untimely death of many a good man.

You cannot avoid going into shock, but you can

do some things to "trick your mind" into remaining calmer and more alert.

The first thing is maintaining a singular *focus* on something other than the perceived threat. Maybe it is the child next to you; maybe it is the sound of police sirens in the background; maybe it is a prayer. It ultimately does not matter. Focus on something more *positive* than the present fear.

The second thing is surprisingly simple but highly effective: breathing. Remember, so much of what you are feeling is purely physiological. All sorts of hormones are being pumped through your system. So just breathe. Here's how to do it.

**Breathe deeply**—Most anxious breaths are fast and shallow, but you should reach deeper into your lungs and make your belly move while breathing. This ensures deep breaths that engage the diaphragm.

**Breathe slowly**—Rapid and erratic breaths only increase what the experts call your "parasympathetic" response. Consciously slowing your breaths will calm your body down almost immediately.

**Breathe coherently**—Panicked breaths are, by definition, anything but coherent. They are fast, shallow, staggered, etc. Coherent breathing (especially in an emergency) requires serious thought and control.

The goal is to breathe (i.e., take breaths in and out) at a rate of about five cycles per minute. Inhale through your nose slowly and deeply (count to six or so), and then exhale through your mouth at about the same rate.

Why don't you just stop and practice it now? Focus on something positive and breathe deeply for a minute or two. You will probably see that even in a non-emergency situation, this practice positively affects the mind and body.

The strangest thing about the state of shock might be time distortion. For some, mere seconds seem like an eternity. For others, hours are distilled into a single moment. Forgetting entire blocks of time is also common.

This, thinking back to a previous topic—should I stay or go?—is sometimes what makes that final decision so difficult. Let us now proceed to some things to consider when it comes to this big question: Should I come out of hiding or not?

# When the Smoke Clears

This, of course, is a proverbial way of saying, "The threat has been addressed, and the scene is now safe."

Obviously, that exact announcement is probably *not* going to be aired over loudspeakers, but there are several ways in which this message can be communicated.

First of all, there is radio. My wife and kids tease me about it all the time, but I typically carry a radio, and some of the saved channels monitor emergency response teams. If I hear the phrase "Code 4," I immediately know that the police are in control of the situation. No other assistance is needed.

I know you probably don't want to join the club of tech nerds that carry radios at this point, so here are some other options for you. And guess what? It still comes back to radios!

If you are concealed, stay there until you can hear the background chatter of radio communication. The police, firefighters, and medics will probably be talking with one another, which is a reasonably reliable sign that they are in control of the scene.

Many emergency response teams will also call out, "Does anyone need help? Is there anyone in need of medical attention?" An attacker might also use this line to call out more prey, so carefully peek out of cover before responding.

If you are convinced that the smoke has indeed settled and you trust that a team is ready to ensure your safety, you can come out of cover. But be *intensely* safe as you do so!

The safest thing to do is to stay put and call for help. If you arise out of cover unexpectedly, there is always a chance that you will be mistaken as a threat.

Also, remember that the police do not know who you are or what you intend. Show them your hands, move slowly, and wait to receive commands.

If the situation truly has ended, you have all the time in the world to be recognized and rescued.

This reminds me of something I should have mentioned about our involuntary biological responses. Forget about using the restroom in an emergency situation. Even the most hardened soldiers soil themselves when things are FUBAR (look up that acronym at your own risk, ladies). Seriously, don't give it a second thought. No one will judge you.

# Section Two:
# Practicum

Thank you for taking the time to learn the basic principles of preparedness. Not everyone does, but those who do are exceedingly more likely to survive a public shooting situation.

Like I said earlier, if you *really* master the principles, you should be able to write all of the entries that follow.

As promised in the introduction, I visited all the places my family regularly goes with a clipboard in hand. I often spoke with a manager or employee to determine the best cover in each location and accessible opportunities to exit the premises without undue notice. I also added a few places my family does not frequent because my initial reviewers asked me to.

I live in the upper Midwest of the United States, and the towns here tend to be on the smaller size (i.e., populations of 15,000 or less). That means the following audit of properties will probably not seem that helpful to you if you live in a metropolitan area with a million other people.

However, the *principles* that lie behind these assessments always remain the same. They remain applicable in almost every situation. Adapt as needed.

# Airplanes

I hate to handle this location first because it rates *extremely* low on the personal safety chart. Alphabetical order dictates it, however, so here we go.

By rating it "extremely low" on safety, I do not mean to imply that airplanes are inherently unsafe. They are very safe, and (especially since 9/11) the chances of someone getting a gun past security are minimal.

But this is a book about public shootings, and if someone opens fire in an airplane cabin while you are cruising at 35,000 feet, you are pretty much doomed.

The reason, of course, is that most commercial airliners offer nowhere to go and nowhere to hide.

That said, and without giving up all hope, let me highlight at least a few possible options for cover.

The seat in front of you is cover, but it may not stop a bullet. There is plenty of luggage in the overhead compartments (if you have the opportunity to access them). Stacked suitcases can make a semi-decent barricade.

There are also some less obvious opportunities for improvised cover. Remember my comment about an iPad stopping a bullet? Perhaps you should keep one in your carry-on.

Finally, and without intending to be inappropriately morbid: Dead bodies usually stop bullets. If someone begins shooting on an airplane, people are going to die. The quarters are just too close to anticipate no casualties. So, if it comes down to it, cover yourself with a fallen comrade. There is no sacrilege in it.

In a similar vein (and I have not mentioned this yet), *playing dead* is also a legitimate and surprisingly effective option for avoiding an attack. Some call it "playing possum" because that's how the Virginia Opossum survives most attacks.

As I said, airplanes rank pretty low on the public

shooting safety scale, so do what you can. Do what you need to do, and don't feel bad about it.

# Aldi

These stores are small, and they are designed for the efficiency of product stocking and customer flow.

Most of the floor is used for extended shelves made of relatively weak metal, which hold primarily non-dense food items (i.e., items that would not stop a bullet).

The main floor offers some opportunities for concealment, but you will need to look elsewhere for avenues of escape or safe places to hide.

In a crisis, you need to move to the side of the store with all the coolers. There, you will find several options. Let me give a few examples.

**Compactor**—There appeared to be only one main entrance to the warehouse area, and the employee I asked would not let me look in. More on that in a minute.

Through the big double doors, however, I could see a cardboard compactor. Being the first thing to see, one might ignore it and try to move in further, but these machines provided excellent cover.

Not only are they bulletproof, but they are shaped like dumpsters, so you could jump in and cover yourself with an already-flattened box (breaking down the boxes is the employees' job).

Beyond this excellent cover, the warehouse extended to the left and the right. To the left was a walk-in freezer for frozen foods. It was small and unnoteworthy as a place to hide. To the right, however, were many better options.

**Dairy**—These products were stocked in a walk-in cooler, which was relatively tight but had room enough to stock the milk gallons two pallets deep. That's twelve gallons of liquid between you and a bullet—more than sufficient.

**Receiving**—I'm not sure if the dairy cooler connects to the receiving department or if it only shares a hallway. After examining the outside of the building, I confirmed that it contained everything you would expect (steel shelves, steel doors, a semi-trailer, and dumpsters outside).

The only "trick" here is that there is minimal indication of any of these options visible inside the store. This led me to ask an employee about the store's layout. This experience proved instructive enough to include here (especially in the almost-first location audit, thanks again to the tyranny of alphabetical order).

Here was my rehearsed speech: "Good morning. My name is Christian, and I'm writing a book on public safety." If acknowledged, I would continue, "The main focus is on public shootings, so what's the safest place in the store? Where would *you* go if you heard gunfire?"

The woman I approached during this particular audit seemed friendly enough and quickly answered, "I don't know, the bathroom, I guess." My follow-up was, "Is there a way out of the bathroom?" She said, "No." So, I instinctively responded with a smile, "Well, I guess that's *not* the safest place, then."

Her countenance immediately changed. I could tell. So I tried to wrap it up quickly, asking, "I saw that you have a very safe-looking warehouse area behind the coolers, would it be possible for me to take a quick look?"

She said, "No." So I tried once more, "Are those double doors the fastest way to the receiving area?" Again, she said, "No." So stubborn old me finally took the hint and left.

As I said, I finally found the information I needed through an external inspection of the building, but the exchange left me thinking. Why did I just get stonewalled?

Maybe she was just being secretive, but I sensed she was simply uncomfortable discussing the topic.

That is somewhat understandable, but I don't think we can afford to avoid uncomfortable topics any longer. Maybe I will hand her a copy of my book and thank her for helping me write it.

# Banks

You might assume that banks are the safest places in the world, and they can be (but that's only if you are a bank teller). After all, they get the bullet-proof glass and the "emergency button" under the counter. The rest of us get a big lobby with little to no cover.

This, I assume, is intentional because banks have always been subject to robberies, and the police don't like it when criminals can return fire from behind cover. This is no criticism, just an observation.

While visiting my local bank, I was thankful to see multiple exits. One led into another wing of the building, so it was not marked with a sign, but it was definitely worthy of consideration as a possible escape route.

The furniture in the lobby, office spaces, and conference room did promise *some* cover, but only a little. Mainly just opportunities for concealment.

The most fascinating thing I observed was an open safe door off to the side of the main service counter. Obviously, it was not the "big safe" that holds all the bricks of pure gold, but it was a true walk-in safe, so I decided: That's where I would go to hide.

Other than that, and based on what I have seen, your best option when under attack in a bank is to get out if you can and get down if you can't.

# Bathrooms

In my first draft of this book, I included comments about bathrooms in various locations, but it started getting repetitive, so I decided to include it as a separate entry.

Bathrooms, to be brutally honest, are usually a complete death trap. There is typically only one way in or out and no good hiding places. There is, therefore, very little tactical advantage to entering most bathrooms in an emergency situation.

One notable exception would be entering and then locking the door. Most bathroom doors do *not* have locks, but make a mental note if you find one that does. I have noticed a few single-occupant lavatories that do.

Another option is to carry a *doorstop* in your purse. Remember that triangular chunk of wood that sat on the floor at grandma's house? That's a doorstop. Your husband or son could make you one in a couple of minutes. Carry it in your purse, wedge it under a door, and whoever is on the other side of that door will not be entering.

Many companies even make fancy "tactical" doorstops designed for this purpose. I cannot recommend any specific brands because I have never bought one, but you might want to look into them.

Worst-case scenario? If you are trapped in a bathroom and an attacker is on his way in, don't just lock yourself in a stall and stand on the toilet. The gunman knows that old trick because he saw that movie too!

Try this instead: Set up a decoy to divert his attention. Lock one of the first stalls and then crawl under to the next one. Leave your door ajar, stand on the toilet, and wait. When the attacker kicks the locked door in, sneak out of your stall, kick his back as hard as you can, and run for it.

Oops. I said no fighting earlier in the book, but listen, when caught in a death trap, you need to do what you need to do in order to get out.

# Buses

First, I have a confession to make. There was *no way* I was going to get onto a public bus in order to write this audit. You probably know me well enough by now.

Thankfully, I didn't need to ride an actual bus because my state's "safety statutes" are posted online. In addition, many bus manufacturers also have safety tutorial videos posted online for their drivers to watch. To the details, then.

Generally speaking, buses present the same main problem as airplanes. Namely, that there are just not many good places to hide. Unlike planes, however, buses are required by law to have *plenty* of accessible emergency exits.

**School Bus**—Know your exits, get down, and get out if possible.

Tell your children to look for red handles and emergency labels, which should be found on both the main door and the rear doors.

Sometimes, specific windows can be swung open in an emergency. There will also probably be an emergency hatch on the ceiling in case of a rollover.

One little-known fact that applies to most buses is this: the front windshield (i.e., the largest window on the bus) is designed to be kicked out in an emergency situation. Use all your weight, lead with your foot, and don't worry about the glass shattering. It should fall out in one piece.

**City Bus**—These are essentially the same as school buses, so again, just look for red handles and labels. Some will also have a side door in addition to the front and rear exits.

Remember also what we learned about hooligans. Quickly scan the bus before committing to the ride. Don't get on if it is filled with people who don't look safe. It's really that simple. Your boss will probably excuse your tardiness if you explain the situation. You can even blame it on my book if you want.

**Coach Bus**—The Federal Department of Regulations requires similar safety measures to those already mentioned so, again, just look for red levers and labels.

A little repetition also never hurts, so I will say it once again: Get out if you can. Get down if you can't. Play dead if you must. Just stay alive.

# Churches

There are many different kinds of churches, so this particular audit threatened to become excessively long. However, there are essentially only two *main types* of church buildings: classic and modern. We will limit our attention to a sample of each category.

**Classic**—This category includes old Catholic cathedrals and the many Lutheran and Presbyterian buildings our grandfathers and great-grandfathers built.

These buildings almost uniformly consist of a foyer, an auditorium, and back rooms behind the pulpit. Of course, various church traditions have fancy names for all these spaces, but that is beyond the scope of our interest.

People don't spend much time in the foyer, so

let's skip to the auditorium (some call it the sanctuary). Wooden pews are now your best friend. Not only can they provide complete cover, but some might even stop a bullet. So get down and hide under them if you ever hear gunfire.

Consider also what might be in those rooms behind the pulpit and where they might lead. Most shooters will enter through the main doors, which places the threat behind you. You could plan to sit up front so you could sneak into one of those rooms if necessary. At the very least, the pastor will be impressed.

The cathedral I attended as a child had those back rooms, which provided all sorts of places to hide. There was also an exit to the back parking lot.

Spend some time running mental scenarios the next time you are not paying attention to the homily or sermon. God will most likely forgive you.

**Modern**—Modern churches are generally a mess, not just aesthetically but also in terms of tactical advantage. The bigger ones are laid out like movie theaters or concert halls (those are some of the least safe spaces imaginable).

I did not visit any modern church buildings on a Sunday morning because I am a minister and need to be at my church every week, but I did watch some livestream services and drove through a few parking lots to verify my suspicions.

Many modern churches do not have an exit behind the pulpit area, so don't bother trying to exit through those doors. They are probably just closets. No sign means no outside access, and some church floor designs essentially leave you trapped in the auditorium.

Worse, wooden pews have largely been replaced with cushy chairs, which are definitely not bulletproof. They still provide an opportunity for concealment, so getting down and staying down is still a legitimate option.

Other than that, I'm not sure what other information to share that might keep you safe.

The limitations of modern church design are real and are one of the main reasons my local church developed an armed response plan. Ask your minister if such a plan exists in your congregation, and if it doesn't, let him know I am willing to visit the location and help the church leadership develop one.

Our church safety plan keeps it very simple for the people: When you hear someone yell, "Drop your weapon!" get down on the ground, call 911 if you can, and don't move until a trusted voice says, "All clear."

# Concert Venues

In the previous church audit, I alluded to the fact that concert venues rank very low on the personal safety scale. If you have been to a concert, you probably know why.

"Pack people in" seems to be the philosophy behind most concert venue floor plans, and this leaves you, as one of the crowd, extremely vulnerable in a shooting situation.

Worse, if you decide to make the "Get down and stay down" move, it might leave you trampled to death by a hundred people who just decided to run in every direction.

So what should you do? Look for exits in the opposite direction of the threat, and consider your ability to move through the crowd and make it there.

Also, here is an insider tip: Band equipment can function very well as improvised cover.

I played in bands when I was young, and I therefore know how much heavy junk we hauled to each concert. For example, the speaker cabinet I used for my guitar was made from three-quarter-inch plywood. It was definitely a bullet-stopper.

Also, if the venue is versatile, there may be a band pit under the stage. In most venues, there is at least a backstage where all the equipment is initially loaded. You just found another exit.

Just run some mental scenarios before the lights are dimmed and the smoke machines start. It will serve you well.

# Doctors' Offices

I'm sitting down to write this entry immediately after a regular check-up. First, the good news: I'm not dying. Now, the bad news: Doctor's offices rank pretty low on the personal safety scale.

The two offices I had the opportunity to survey had two entrances each, so that's good. The main entry is marked, so that is probably where a shooter would enter. The one on the opposite end of the suite was less conspicuous. The whole space was U-shaped, so if a shooter entered one way, you could easily exit the other.

I asked the nurse and the doctor where they would go if they heard gunshots, and they admitted to there not being any good options. There were plenty of desks and a decent-sized table in the breakroom to use for cover, but that was about it.

One thing there was plenty of was the doors. There were more doors than I could count, and I cannot imagine a shooter checking every single one in search of a target. Pick an inconspicuous one if you plan to hide (e.g., linens, technology, etc.).

While I was sitting in the very small exam room, I found only one safe place to hide. This is definitely an old trick, but it is an effective one.

As previously discussed, most shooters are on the move and looking for targets of opportunity. If one walked by my room and saw the light on and the door closed, they *might* take a second to see if anyone was there.

So here's what you might do (it is a little counterintuitive): Turn the lights off, make sure no personal effects are visible, open the door as wide as it will go, and stand quietly behind it.

Even if the shooter steps in, he will not see you. You will see the muzzle of his rifle, by the way, which offers you an opportunity to disarm the attacker, but that's more fighting, so let's save that for another book—shall we?

# Farm and Fleet

Farm and Fleet is a typical "big box" store. Based on its name, you would think it would be filled with plenty of heavy-duty opportunities for cover. Not so.

Most of the main floor is filled with shelving units that don't look very strong and don't go up very high. There would be no benefit in trying to climb up and hide anywhere.

Also, most of the products were not dense enough to stop a bullet. There were, however, some feed bags and larger boxes that would provide decent cover.

The key to finding safety options in this store is to locate the exterior walls. Each one has a "hidden" area with ample possibilities for cover or escape.

**The front**—There was a second story above

customer service and the cashier area. It had windows with one-way mirrors, so I assume that is where the managers and security personnel work.

It would not be my first choice for cover (because being upstairs, there would be no way out), but most shooters tend not to venture into obscure areas like this.

**Side # 1**—Behind a wall with huge signs reading "Women" and "Kids," there was a warehouse area filled with all the typical sources of cover (steel shelves, pallets, etc.), but it was relatively small.

**The back**—Equally unimpressive was the small space behind the "Sports & Outdoors" wall. Don't get me wrong, I would rather be in there than on the main floor, but then I found the store's true sanctuary.

**Side # 2**—This is where you will find the "Car Care" department, which provides a wide variety of high-quality cover. You could climb steel shelving units, hide behind boxes or a rack of tires, or simply exit the building into the back lot.

You might also remember this as an example of how to complete an easy and memorable audit. All you need to remember for Farm and Fleet is this, "Exterior walls is where I will find cover."

By the way, you should say things like that to your kids on occasion (especially when a building is that simple). It can even sound cute, "Farm and Fleet? Flee to the side."

# Fast Food Restaurants

We have plenty of these around town, and I walked through several of them (McDonald's, Burger King, KFC, and my personal favorite, Culver's).

Most of these buildings are the same, and rank pretty low on a personal safety scale.

The amount of windows, for example, is a mixed blessing. Yes, they enable you to see what's happening outside and who is about to enter the building, but they also mean you are highly visible as a potential target.

I considered the tables as potential cover, but many were bolted to the floor, which would prevent you from knocking them on their side. The tabletops were also made of particle board rather than plywood, so they are definitely not bullet-proof.

One good feature of these buildings is that there are several exits. You can usually enter from both sides and, though you cannot see it, there is also a rear exit behind the kitchen area. This is where the low man on the totem pole takes the trash out to the dumpster. This is also where I would head if I had opportunity.

Most of the time, though, a fast food incident will involve robbery. This leaves all the focus on the front counter, so you may not be able to sneak out through the kitchen.

Like I said, fast food restaurants rank relatively low on the personal safety scale.

If there is a play area out front, I recommend dining there. It is in a separate room from the order counter; there is an emergency exit and plenty of places for you and your children to hide (e.g., slides, tunnels, etc.).

Other than that, my advice, as usual, is this: Get out if you can and get down if you can't.

# Gas Stations

The gas station my family frequents most often is relatively small, so think more in terms of a mini-mart rather than a truck stop.

Besides selling fuel, there is a nice little convenience store attached to it that sells milk, eggs, frozen meat, baked goods, etc.

While I like the quality of locally sourced products, the store itself ranks extremely low in terms of personal safety. There is nowhere to go and nowhere to hide.

There is only one main entrance. The bathrooms are, as expected, a dead end. The walk-in cooler might work for concealment, but it is a pretty tight space. All the cabinets were too small for even a child to enter.

Yes, there was a "back room" that led to an

emergency exit, but it was very small and cluttered. Don't plan to hide in a room like that. Just get out.

This is simply one of the risks you face when it comes to gas stations and small convenience stores. So again, I don't blame the owners at all. Even the manager I spoke with admitted, "There's really nowhere to hide, so I would just try to get out."

She guessed that the main counter "might be strong enough to stop a bullet" and added that there was an emergency button beneath the register.

Upon exiting the building, I did notice a dumpster and some large bins for rubbish and recycling outside, but not much else.

Other than that, I think places like this make a very good case for the "pay at the pump" option.

I suggest grocery shopping at a place that is less likely to become a war zone over a pack of cigarettes and a few hundred bucks.

My wife, in fact, has occasionally gone without milk in the morning because of loitering hooligans spotted outside the store. Do you remember my earlier observation about disappointing those we love? Safety sometimes requires it. What would my children rather have: Milk in their cereal or mom safely at home?

# Grocery Stores

We have a huge grocery store in town. So before going in, I drove around the building to see how many emergency exits I should expect to locate once inside.

You should take the time to do that, especially if it's a store you visit every week. It will provide you with an entirely new "lay of the land" than that to which your mind is already accustomed.

Once inside the store, as expected, there were several emergency exits, and I was happy to see them all clearly marked. Some, however, needed to be accessed by walking through doors ordinarily used only by employees. Most customers ignore these areas most of the time.

I spoke with a manager and asked, "Where is the safest place in this building? Where would you go if you heard gunfire right now?" He confirmed my suspicion by pointing to the one area none of the customers ever see. They call it the "back room."

That term is a colloquial catch-all phrase for areas commonly called the receiving dock, warehouse, mechanical room, and walk-in coolers. Upon inspection, I agree this is indeed the safest area in the store, so let's start there.

Behind the clean and tidy façade of most retail presentations is a huge, less presentable area filled with all sorts of cover. Here are some of the most noteworthy things I saw while touring the "back room."

**The Back**—Besides steel exit doors and a forklift, there was plenty of steel shelving that would be easy enough to climb and stand upon. The shelves themselves were not the prime cover, but the pallets of product upon them.

I noticed that you could also step right from the shelves onto the roof of one of the massive walk-in coolers. I could not see what was up there, but that's the whole point, right?

Through the steel exit doors, there was also a variety of heavy-duty cover: dumpsters, a cardboard compactor, a semi-trailer, etc.

So when thieves start making noise up front by the registers, go the opposite way. Find the "back room." It is truly that simple.

**Other Rooms**—I walked the inside perimeter of the building first because looking down long central aisles for cover is about as productive as looking down long hallways. Don't waste your time.

This perimeter is where all the emergency exit signs were posted. One led first through a kitchen, but I couldn't see much of it. I'm sure there were cabinets, carts, ovens, etc. – all possible hiding spots.

Another exit led through the butcher's area, which I could see into somewhat. There were, as expected, plenty of stainless steel surfaces and a walk-in freezer.

One very inconspicuous room was actually up front, spanning the whole length of the store. The windows were one-way glass, so they looked like mirrors. This is where the surveillance people work, and a few offices are also up there.

This area could be accessed through two doors leading to staircases, but neither was marked. That's understandable because only employees (i.e., the managers) use these doors with any frequency.

While discussing this area with one manager, I asked whether the security people who work up there are armed. He said they were not and guessed that the response time for local police was about ten minutes. Not bad.

Regarding alerting authorities, the cashiers have an emergency button under the counter. Go ahead and borrow it if you need to.

**The Sales Floor**—This is where all the coverless aisles are arranged in straight lines. I checked the shelving units; none were large enough to crawl onto and cover yourself with product. Forget about them.

One item of interest on the sales floor was pallets of products staged as featured or discounted items. Depending on the featured product, these would be excellent for cover and might even stop a bullet.

The only other thing that caught my eye were the large stand-alone freezers and coolers. Some were even arranged back-to-back, so there was a small space in between—another potential hiding spot.

Obviously, not all of these coolers would stop a bullet, but what kind of nut job is going to shoot a Tombstone pizza just for fun? Actually, I'll take that back. I'm sure there are plenty nowadays.

Think, though, about those frozen chest coolers. One that I saw was filled with meat, and the last time I checked, frozen meat is as hard as ice. A foot of frozen meat should stop (or at least deflect) a bullet.

You will have to do your own personal audit of the grocery store you frequent most often, but many of these features will prove common enough.

# Hospitals

If you want to stay safe in a hospital, you are going to face a lot of the same challenges as those trapped in a school. I wrote the "schools" chapter first, so you might want to flip ahead and come back to this entry.

My main concern about hospitals is that long corridors with no cover are inherently unsafe. Nevertheless, that is the main terrain. I worked in a hospital for over seven years, so I have at least a few "secrets" to share.

Forget about hiding in hallways and hospital rooms—they are death traps. What you need to do is find those inconspicuous spaces that only employees use.

One of the most readily convenient is laundry rooms. They are just big closets, but they provide a couple of distinct benefits. One is gondolas, which are big bins that hold linens. They provide a very nondescript means of concealment.

The other thing is the laundry chute. It looks big enough to accommodate an average-sized person and leads to a whole different level of the building. If you choose this option of escape, you should probably grab a laundry bag first to slow your descent and break your fall.

Two other areas of the hospital that offer distinct advantages are the cafeteria and the warehouse. They are usually located on the same level because they both have a receiving area where trucks deliver supplies.

The cafeteria leads to a kitchen, and I already suggested some of the cover you can expect to find there (e.g., cabinets, freezers, stainless steel countertops, etc.).

Receiving areas provide even better opportunities for cover because of their discreet location and other bonuses, such as pallets of material, steel skid loaders, cardboard compactors, and huge doors that lead to the outside world.

You may not be able to find these areas once inside, so do yourself a favor and drive around the block once before entering. Take mental notes of the signs that say "receiving," "deliveries," or "truck traffic." Knowing these locations could save your life.

# Libraries

The great thing about libraries is that they are filled with books, and walls of books are basically bullet-proof. Besides that, libraries are not designed with tactical safety in mind.

I took a minute to enter "Library shooting" into an internet search engine, and it yielded only scant results for shootings that occurred *inside* public libraries.

Most reported incidents occurred *outside*, which is just another reminder that hooligans tend to haunt public spaces.

Anyway, let's get to brass tacks. There are emergency exits, desks to hide beneath, copiers to hide behind, study rooms to enter, and plenty of books to stop bullets. But here is one more item to store in your mental arsenal: higher ground.

Remember, most active shooters have tunnel vision. They tend not to look up, so consider climbing a bookshelf like a ladder and lying quietly on top. Yes, the shelving unit *will* hold your weight, and the shooter will not be able to see you.

# Menards

This audit, to be embarrassingly honest, was a dream come true. Anyone with the natural tendency to run mental safety scenarios should spend an hour at Menards. It will prove *deeply* satisfying.

That being said, I don't want this audit to be much longer than the others, so let me break it down rather quickly (and in a way that seeks to stimulate your imagination).

**Shelves**—Almost all the shelving units in the store are heavy duty, and many hold large boxes that would provide complete concealment.

Most shelves looked easy enough to climb, and at the top of some were surprisingly excellent places to hide. Imagine hiding in a porcelain bathtub twenty feet in the air!

Many shelves were also deep and sat relatively

close to the ground. I observed some in the back of the building that employees had parked flatbed carts under. What a great place to crawl under to hide!

Materially-dense products were also plentiful on the shelves. Items like ceramic tile, hardwood flooring, and even five-gallon buckets of paint would definitely slow, if not stop, a bullet.

**Upstairs**—This feature is unique to Menards (at least insofar as I have seen amongst other big box stores). It is crafted of steel and concrete, freely open to public access, and usually overlooked by patrons.

It spans much of the central main floor, but in two main sections is connected by a catwalk. You will find the same cover upstairs as you did on the main floor (i.e., steel shelving units with products stacked).

One interesting feature I found at Menards, which most retail stores lack nowadays, is an elevator, so let's give this excellent cover option the attention it deserves.

**Elevators**—Upon first glance, they might look like a dead end, but they are much more than that. Once inside, you can not only leave a dangerous scene for a safer one, but you can even suspend yourself in nearly perfect cover by using the "emergency stop" button.

Time your stop well enough and the elevator will halt between two floors (with all the benefits of having steel and concrete all around you). Another advantage is that this will automatically engage an emergency alarm, which alerts everyone else in the building to the fact that code red is now in effect.

A two-way communication device is also required in many states, automatically connecting you to personnel trained for emergency responses.

**The Yard**—This is the "outside" part of the store and is definitely the safest place of all. Not only does it contain *heavier-duty* steel shelves than those inside, but most of the inventory stored there is beyond bulletproof.

There are racks of lumber and plywood, pallets of brick and stone, forklifts and trucks, dumpsters and trailers, and all sorts of nooks and crannies between, which could accommodate full-grown adults and their entire family.

You do have to purchase products from the yard in order to enter with a vehicle, but you can walk right out into it from inside the building (i.e., through the garden center or in the back where they sell building supplies).

**Miscellaneous**—You should really do a walk-through yourself, and as you do, here are a few more things to watch for: carpet remnants leaned against the wall, large cabinets and sheds on display, chest freezers and safes, and entire kitchen displays with empty cabinets. There are all sorts of good places to hide. Menards takes the prize for the safest place to shop!

# Movie Theaters

I previously mentioned the movie theater floor plan when evaluating modern churches. I still have nothing good to say about it. For the most part, a movie theater is a death trap.

At the same time, I can mention a few things that might help you survive a shooting in a cinema.

First, your emergency exits are usually near the screen. Mentally mark those as you take your seat. The problem with that, of course, is that no one likes to sit near the front of the theater, making it hard to access the exits in an emergency.

I don't go out to see many movies. I prefer to watch them while in code white (i.e., while reclining on my couch). I'll wait six months for that. But on the rare occasion I have attended the cinema, I prefer to sit in the back. The back row is, in my opinion, the best.

Not only do you avoid the risk of having annoying people behind you, but the last row becomes quickly eclipsed into a shooter's peripheral vision as he enters the theater. Even with only a few steps into the room, you are now behind him, and his eyes are probably focused down the barrel of his rifle.

Any movement will automatically focus his sight elsewhere, so use that to your advantage as the crowd in front of you begins running amok. If you can sneak out, do so. If not, get down and pull the chair seat down with your hand to conceal your body.

# Parades

"I love a parade!" so the old song goes. But remember, it was written in the 1930s, and that was definitely a different time.

My family attends the annual parade in our town, and I noticed something different last summer. School buses were parked across all the streets leading to the town square, and I immediately knew why.

About six months prior, you see, there was a man in our state who killed six people and injured sixty-two others by driving his car into a public parade.

I asked the police about the buses, and they confirmed that it was a new precautionary measure. I was very thankful for it.

Parades have become dangerous, and we need

to face that fact. That does not mean we should stop attending them, but we must be more mindful and prepared.

I have already described all the types of cover you will find on a typical main street. Take a mental note of them and use them if necessary. Set up your chairs, for example, next to one of those huge concrete planters.

One thing I have yet to mention is the usefulness of storefront businesses. Some of them have recessed entryways. If possible, sit near one of those. It will afford you accessible and effective cover in a crisis, even if the business is closed.

Better yet, sit in front of a business that has chosen to remain open for the parade. If anything bad happens, you can run through the front doors and find cover, or just keep running until you find the back door and exit the entire situation.

If you cannot make such plans in advance and find yourself exposed, take a look at the parade vehicles themselves. There will usually be plenty of large trucks pulling steel trailers with parade floats mounted upon them. Hide in or under one of them if needed.

# Schools

First of all, let it be acknowledged that a school shooting is a mother's worst nightmare. When I was young, such a thing did not even exist. Today, that nightmare has become a horrid reality.

Millions of moms escort their children to the bus every single day. It is an act of high trust. They have taught their children to obey their teachers, and they have chosen to trust those teachers to watch over their little ones while they are away from home.

Thankfully, most schools in this country have adopted a very specific set of protocols for shooting events and diligently train the teachers and students to follow them.

At the same time, it is *your* responsibility as a

parent to empower your children to stay safe when protocols prove to be imperfect.

The most common school safety protocol goes under the moniker "Run, Hide, Fight," and it is not that bad. Let's consider it applied to a school building.

**Run**—That, of course, is always a good option *if* you have somewhere to go. Schools are designed to maximize student traffic flow, so the main architectural feature is hallways. I already told you what I think about hallways. Don't run down one if you can help it.

When I attended grammar school, we were taught to break a window in the classroom for an emergency exit. I remember some windows even had knock-out panels beneath them made from some kind of composite material.

If you hear gunshots in the hallway, exit through the window if necessary. Your teacher may not be initially pleased with your action, but she will probably follow you as the gunshots start sounding closer.

**Hide**—We have spent a lot of time learning about options for cover, and this is where most schools rank very high in at least one area. There is a lot of concrete. Again, though, concrete corridors do not provide ideal cover. Neither do offices and classrooms.

There was a school shooting about a year ago, and I watched the video footage. The shooter walked slowly down the hall and peeked into rooms as she passed them. She was looking for a target. She was looking for movement. So, if you are going to hide, try for total concealment.

Some classrooms have storage cabinets, all offices have desks, and bleachers have open space beneath. Cafeterias lead to kitchens, which contain all sorts of steel structures. Libraries have books that create bulletproof walls. Auditoriums have band pits and wardrobe closets.

Run some mental scenarios next time you are not paying attention in class. Your mom won't mind—that's why she handed you this book (hint, hint, moms). Maybe you could even write a book report on it for extra credit.

**Fight**—I understand why the experts include this option, but it can't be emphasized enough that this is truly a *last resort* option when your opponent has a firearm.

Remember, public shooters are looking for

targets. They are looking for movement. So if you stand up and throw a book, you are probably going to get shot. Just stay down instead.

If you truly are *forced* to fight, be smart about it and attack the shooter from a position where *you* have the advantage.

Remember, most people don't look up unless they need to, so find higher ground, wait until the threat passes by, and let the fire extinguisher do the work as you fall upon your enemy's head. Yes, that sounds awful, but at least you are still alive. Welcome to the modern jungle.

# Walmart

Walmart stores are, in one sense, architectural masterpieces. Framed in steel and using open web joists, the vast openness of their retail space provides for absolute flexibility in interior organization.

That's the only good thing I have to say about this particular location.

The main floor is obviously organized for retail sales with endless aisles of affordable products. None of that, however, was of interest to me. I was there for a safety audit.

The main floor offered *no* good opportunities for cover. The shelves appeared weak; they were not very tall, and most of the products stored on them were very low density. They might work for concealment, but that's about it.

The only structure on the main floor that looked bulletproof was in the back, where they sold electronics. Due to the modern societal scourge of unchecked shoplifting, all the phones and games were locked in steel cages. The service desk, interestingly enough, was also made of steel. Back of the building? Made of steel? Not bad.

The area outside the retail space was of much greater interest to me. Several doors led there, many of which were marked as exits, so I took a peek inside.

Once inside, you can essentially circumnavigate the entire building while enjoying a whole pallet of stock between you and the retail space (at least most of the time). Steel doors that led to the outside were also plentiful.

There were main receiving docks on both back corners, along with an entirely separate area for car care (all of which offered the standard options for industrial cover, which surely you know by now).

My unauthorized tour quickly ended as I approached the bakery area because there were too many people around, and I didn't want to get in any trouble.

Interestingly, only *one* employee took notice of

me the whole time I was in the store. Everyone else was seemingly oblivious.

I mean, come on! A guy is walking around without a shopping cart, with a notepad and pen in hand, looking up, down, and all around, and only one guy noticed? By the way, I gave him the "I see you too" nod to break the tension, and it quickly did.

There is one last thing about the building that intrigued me but remains a mystery: the front wall.

Like most retail stores, it appeared that there might be a second floor behind the cashier stations. But there were no one-way mirrors for surveillance.

Not seeing any obvious entrances to this area, I went to customer service and engaged an employee with my well-rehearsed introduction. Then, I asked plainly, "Are there any rooms above you?" She said, "No."

When I asked her where she would go in an emergency, she unconsciously glanced to the left and said, "I'd probably go into the cash offices." What are those? *Where* are those? She was clearly not going to divulge.

Sensing her discomfort with the conversation, I

concluded with a smile, "I told you that I had a few strange questions to ask." She graciously replied, "No question is strange if someone thinks to ask it." I couldn't agree more.

If something catches your attention while conducting an audit, go ahead and ask about it. If people seem secretive, mark it in your mind as something worth investigating in a crisis.

Walmart—what an interesting experience! I would say avoid it if you can, and if you can't, stay alert and run for the warehouse that wraps around the side with all the groceries.

# Epilogue

To close, let me briefly address two anticipated —and completely understandable—complaints you might have against this book.

I encountered the first from my wife as she read my first draft. It wasn't a formal complaint but more of an excited, "Oh, what about this place? What about that place?"

Yes, I could have added more locations to the practicum section, but there are already twice as many as I had initially planned.

My goal in writing this book was not to provide an encyclopedia but simply to establish some universally applicable principles of survival.

More than that, I don't even need to visit *every* business in the country because if you have mastered the principles in section one and started to notice some repetitive advice in section two, congratulations! You are now more than capable of completing your own safety audits.

The other anticipated complaint is certainly related but far less straightforward to resolve: "What about people who live in urban areas? This book might work fine for moms living in the quiet Midwest, but what about those who live in a bustling metropolis with a million other people?"

First of all, while I might admit that the practicum section may be of *limited* value to such moms, the principles taught in section one are *universally* applicable in any environment.

There are trees and hedges in Central Park, plenty of concrete structures in Chicago, and lots of dumpsters in Denver. I can assure you that there is plenty of cover to be found in your city.

Here's the real problem: statistically speaking, crime rates are always higher in cities, and that simply puts you at a higher risk of danger if you choose to adopt the urban lifestyle.

By all means, do your best to stay safe, but let me be bold enough to raise what should be an obvious question. Do you really need to live in such a high-risk environment?

I never could because I take personal safety way

too seriously. My mind would eventually break after running so many scenarios every single day.

Remember, you should be able to live in yellow all day long. Most urban environments prevent that possibility. They effectively force you into condition orange every time you leave your apartment.

Consider your capacity for such sustained mental alertness before moving to a city. If you already live in a city and no longer feel safe, seriously consider relocation.

There are plenty of communities left in America that have never been disrupted by a public shooting event and which likely never will. Smaller generally means safer.

Thinking back to that mom who "just started running" after hearing those gunshots at the parade, I would love to have been her neighbor. But then again, she is my neighbor in at least some respect, and so are you. That is why I wrote this book.

Thank you so much for taking the time to read it. I hope you have learned much about situational awareness and specific strategies to keep yourself and your loved ones safe in a public shooting situation.

Trust me, if you have mastered the basic principles in this book, you are far better equipped than most people to survive a dangerous situation.

If, on the other hand, all this information has your mind somewhat reeling, simply reread section one. I kept the book short on purpose. I also included a handy "cheat sheet" on the last page so you can occasionally review the principles with your children.

Well, I guess that's about it. If I happen to see you out there in the real world and catch you scanning the room, don't be surprised (or alarmed!) if I shoot you a quick smile. Let's count it as a precious moment shared in code yellow and move on with our wonderfully safe lives.

# Cheat Sheet

"Cheat sheets" are rightly forbidden during exams, but this is not school. This is real life, and remembering what you have learned in this book might save your life someday.

Therefore, a brief outline is offered on the next page to assist your memory and facilitate group discussion amongst family and friends. Feel free to copy that page and use it in any educational setting.

In fact, if you would like to purchase multiple copies of this book for use in a book discussion group, Sunday school class, homeschooling co-op, or some other educational setting, contact the publisher to receive a quantity discount. The website address is on the last page of the book.

## Mental Condition

- White: Happy oblivion
- Yellow: Relaxed awareness
- Orange: Focused awareness
- Red: Immediate Response

## Response Actions

- Get down now!
- Alert the authorities
- Find some cover
- Get out if you can

## Utilizing Cover

- Natural (dirt, trees)
- Man-made (steel, timber)
- Improvised (iPad, smoke)
- Know the varying degrees

## Time to Hide

- Do I stay or go?
- Shock sets in
- Stay sly as a fox
- The smoke clears

Christian M. McShaffrey was born in the South, raised in the Midwest, and then moved further North to start a family and plant a church. He and his wife Kelly are raising the younger of their six children on a quiet—and very safe—homestead just outside of town.

When not working at church or at home, Christian enjoys a variety of hobbies, such as hunting, fishing, pistolcraft, sailing, music, and (obviously) writing.

He manages or is a member of several organizations: Kept Pure Press LLC (owner), Text & Translation webzine (editor-in-chief), The Bahnsen Institute (vice-chairman), Reformation Bible Society (secretary), Presbytery of Wisconsin and Minnesota (stated clerk), Wisconsin Department of Natural Resources (volunteer hunter safety instructor), and Seminario Reformado de las Américas (board of visitors).

Christian has traveled extensively to teach on various topics. He has spoken in Canada, England, Ireland, Scotland, and also in many of our own states (California, Colorado, Illinois, Missouri, Virginia, and Wisconsin).

If you would like to book him for an interview or seminar, use the contact page at the following website:

*aplacetohide.org*

www.ingramcontent.com/pod-product-compliance
Lightning Source LLC
Chambersburg PA
CBHW070531160726
48003CB00004B/1754